mothering
without
guilt

D1403115

Other Studies in A Mom's Ordinary Day Bible Study Series

Jean E. Syswerda is mother to three grown children. A former editor and associate publisher at Zondervan, she was responsible for such best-selling Bibles as the *NIV Adventure Bible*, the *NIV Teen Study Bible*, and the *NIV Women's Devotional Bible 1*. She is the general editor of the *NIV Women of Faith Study Bible* and the *NLT Prayer Bible*, as well as the coauthor of the *Read with Me Bible* and the best-selling *Women of the Bible*.

Sharon Hersh is the mother of two teenagers. She is also a licensed professional counselor, author, and speaker. She is the author of *Bravehearts* and *Mom, I Feel Fat!* She lives with her family in Lone Tree, Colorado.

six sessions

YOU & GOD . YOU & OTHERS . YOU & YOUR KIDS

mom

a mom's ordinary day

BIBLE STUDY SERIES

mothering
without
guilt

**JEAN E.
SYSWERDA**
general editor

written by
**SHARON
HERSH**

We want to hear from you. Please send your comments about this book to us in care of zreview@zondervan.com. Thank you.

Mothering without Guilt
Copyright © 2003 by Jean Syswerda

Requests for information should be addressed to:
Zondervan, *Grand Rapids, Michigan 49530*

ISBN 978-0-310-24715-9

Interior design by Tracey Moran

Printed in the United States of America

contents

how to use this study guide

Hey, Mom, are you ready?

When was the last time you did something just for you?

In the joy and junk and memories and mess that is your life as a mother, do you sometimes feel that you've lost something—something essential and important?

The Bible studies in this series will help you rediscover and, even more, enjoy all the parts and pieces that make you a unique person, a unique mother, and a unique and holy creation of God.

The five sections of each individual session are designed to meet a particular need in your life—the need for time alone, for time with God's Word, for time with others, for time with God, and for time with your children. How you approach and use each section is up to you and your individual styles and desires. But here are a few suggestions:

For You Alone

The operative word here is, of course, *alone.* For moms who rarely even go to the bathroom alone, being alone can seem an almost impossible goal. Perhaps thinking in terms of *quiet* would help. You can do this part of the study in any quiet moments in your home—when kids are sleeping, when they're watching a video, when you're nursing a little one. Any quiet or personal time you can find in your own schedule will work. This part of the study is sometimes serious, sometimes fun, sometimes downright silly. It will prepare your mind for the other sections of the study.

For You and God's Word

Put this study guide, a pen, and your Bible in a favorite place—somewhere you can grab it at any free moment, perhaps in the kitchen or by a favorite chair. Then, when a few spare moments arise, everything you need is right at hand. Each of the six sessions includes a short Bible study for you to complete alone. (This doesn't necessarily mean you have to *be* alone to complete it! My daughter reads her Bible out loud during a morning bath while her infant son sits in his bouncy seat next to her. She gets her Bible read, and he's content with the sound of his mommy's voice.)

For You and Others

The third section of each study is intended for small groups (even just two is a small group!), but if that isn't possible, you *can* complete it alone. Or connect with a friend or neighbor to work through the materials together. If you function as the leader, little preparation is required; you can learn right along with your fellow mothers. The leader is actually more of a facilitator, keeping the discussion on track and your time together moving along. Leadership information on many of the questions in the "For You and Others" section is included at the back of this book, beginning on page 87.

For You and God

The fourth section of each session will guide you in a time of prayer based on the study's topic. Wonder when you'll find time to do this? Prop this book up in your window while doing dishes. God hears the prayers of moms whose hands are in dishwater! Or take it along in the car when picking up a child from an activity. Or use it while nursing an infant. These times of talking to God are precious moments in the life of a mom. And with all the demands on your time, you need to grab these moments whenever you can. Do also try, though, to find a time each day for quiet, concentrated prayer. Your children need their mom to be "prayed up" when she faces each day.

For You and Your Kids

How great is this? A Bible study that includes something for your kids as well as for you! The final section of each session gives suggestions on applying the principles of the study in your kids' lives as well as in your own. The activities are appropriately geared to different ages and range from simple to more complex.

One Important Final Note

Don't presume you have to move through these sessions in any particular order. The order in which they appear in each study is the ideal. Life doesn't always allow the ideal, however. If you start your study with the last section and then go through from back to front, you'll still be fine. Do whatever works best for you and your schedule and for your treasured little (or not-so-little) offspring.

introduction

Find a picture of your children and take a close look at what God has given to you. The gift of your children was not dependent on your parenting skills, your background, or your success in life. In unrestricted, unconditional love, God gave your children to you.

But as a mom, it doesn't take long before guilt begins to creep in. Guilt for not filling out the baby book completely. Guilt for not breast-feeding long enough. Guilt for not making homemade baby food. Guilt for not taking more pictures. Guilt for not signing up for more committees. Guilt for having a messy house. Guilt for using too many baby-sitters.

Guilt lurks in the corners of the living room, bedroom, and kitchen, mocking you whenever you are tempted to believe that God made *you* uniquely for *your* children. Guilt wants to silence any joy over parenting victories or moments of creative mothering. Guilt peers into the eyes of love and menacingly suggests that love is not enough.

This study guide will challenge guilt with an understanding both of God's heart for you and of his creation of your mother's heart. Chapters 1 and 2 look at guilt straight on and reveal a forgiveness that not only covers a multitude of sins but also sets a mother's heart free to love and laugh, create and cuddle, and play and pray with her children. Chapters 3–6 introduce mentors in mothering—biblical women who were real moms with real lives and who modeled the possibilities of mothering without guilt in the midst of diverse and challenging circumstances.

Wherever you are in your mothering, you will have unique experiences and responses as you interact with the material in this study guide. As you confront your own guilt—whether it's over real failures or unrealistic expectations—you will have an infinite number of opportunities to connect with God, the One whose gaze of love banishes all guilt and lights the pathway of mothering without guilt.

Look at that picture of your children again. Can you hear God speak to you personally these words from Scripture?

> *Dear, dear [mothers], I can't tell you how much I long for you to enter this wide-open, spacious life.... The smallness you feel comes from within you. Your lives aren't small,*
> *but you're living them in a small way. I'm speaking as plainly as I can and with great affection.*
> *Open up your lives. Live openly and expansively!*
>
> 2 CORINTHIANS 6:11–13 THE MESSAGE

when guilt is good

> Search me, O God, and know my heart;
> test me and know my anxious thoughts.
> See if there is any offensive way in me,
> and lead me in the way everlasting.
>
> PSALM 139:23–24

For You Alone

When you read the title of this study guide—*Mothering without Guilt*—did longing leap within your heart? Did you think, *"Oh, I want to mother without guilt,"* only to be quickly extinguished by another thought: *"But I feel guilty all the time."* Mothering without guilt is a reality many moms never experience because they can't distinguish between true guilt, which is good, and false guilt, which is a weapon of the enemy. The result? A nagging sense of guilt that becomes a constant and unwelcome companion.

Take a moment to examine your understanding of guilt and its role in your mothering by looking at the following statements. Check each one that applies to you.

Mothering without guilt means:

- ❏ There is a right way and a wrong way to do everything.
- ❏ I should never lose my temper with my children.
- ❏ I should spend at least an hour in prayer and Bible study daily.
- ❏ Everyone likes my children and me.

- ❑ We should always be on time.
- ❑ I should never be discouraged or grouchy.
- ❑ I should always be ready to correct my children when they make a mistake.
- ❑ I should check and double-check my work to make sure it is perfect.
- ❑ My children will never get sick if I am vigilant in taking care of them.
- ❑ I should anticipate problems before they occur.
- ❑ My children should get good grades in school.
- ❑ I can trust God to keep my children safe if I read my Bible every day.
- ❑ I should always make tasty, well-balanced meals that my kids love to eat!
- ❑ The house should be clean every night before I go to bed.
- ❑ My kids never talk back to me.
- ❑ My children always love to go to church.

If you checked any of these boxes, you probably have pockets of *false* guilt in your life and hopes of mothering without guilt seem pretty far-fetched. False guilt dupes you into believing the ideal is possible.

Look back at the list and underline how many times the words "should," "always," and "never" appear. False guilt nags at you with messages of "should" and "always" and "never." False guilt gains a foothold when other people in your life (especially your children) don't live the way you need them to live in order to satisfy your expectations.

Go back and look again at the boxes you checked. This time evaluate each one in light of these three questions:

- Does achieving this goal require that you live perfectly with perfect children?

- Does this goal allow for interruptions, mistakes, or individual personality traits?

- Is this goal dependent on your children conforming to your agenda?

Guilt is like quicksand. You can get stuck in it.

As long as you are tormented by false guilt, true guilt will be difficult to identify. True guilt is a blessing. Just as a pain in the body may be a warning of physical injury or sickness, guilt is an ache in the soul that signals you to examine your heart for sin. When you let go of the "shoulds" and stop evaluating your mothering by how well your children conform to your agenda, you have the opportunity to look beyond the false guilt to the true guilt pointing to sin that needs to be forgiven. You finally have the opportunity to see an *accurate* self-picture. That's when hope for mothering without guilt begins!

For You and God's Word

Begin your study today by reading Psalm 139:23–24.

> Search me, O God, and know my heart;
> test me and know my anxious thoughts.
> See if there is any offensive way in me,
> and lead me in the way everlasting.

The psalmist David penned this intimate, open prayer. Whom do you trust with your every thought, motivation, choice, decision, or action? David laid his life open before God. He wanted God to see him and help him to accurately evaluate his pain and joy, weariness and vitality, selfishness and unselfishness, sin and service. Laying your life open before God makes it possible to move out of the house of fear and guilt into the house of love.

> Guilt can keep mothers narrowly focused on the question "What's wrong with me?" and prevents us from becoming effective agents of personal and social change.
>
> HARRIET LERNER, *THE MOTHER DANCE*

1. As you think about laying your life bare before God, what do you fear?

2. Do you believe that God can lovingly handle all that goes on in your mind and heart? Explain your answer.

When you don't believe God can be trusted, you become defensive, deny your harmful or hurtful ways, and deflect any hope of change. When you believe that God loves you and longs to forgive you and have an intimate relationship with you, you can look courageously at your life and change can become possible.

Honestly ask yourself, "Do I want to defend myself, or am I willing to open my heart to God's gaze?" "Do I want to deny any hurt or harm I may have caused, or will I allow God to evaluate my actions, reveal their consequences, and offer forgiveness?" "Do I blame others or the circumstances, or can I ask God to unveil my responsibility?"

Your ability to examine yourself accurately is wholly dependent on what you believe about God's love and forgiveness.

3. Recall a time when your young child made a foolish or willful mistake. What did you feel for your child?

> *Never was a mother so blind to the faults of her child as our Lord is toward ours.*
>
> DANIEL CONSIDINE, *CONFIDENCE IN GOD*

Do you believe God to be distant, easily annoyed, indifferent, or angry? Is he always watching you so that he can catch you in your sin and punish you? Do you believe that God is harsher with you than you are with your own child? Pray the words of Psalm 139:23–24, focusing on a God who is completely loving and completely trustworthy. Can you bare your heart before him? Can you be honest? Now write out the prayer of Psalm 139 in your own words, and use it throughout the week in your prayer times.

For You and Others

Begin your time together as a small group by discussing this question: *What is the deepest need of the human heart?*

Look back at the boxes you checked in "For You Alone." What do these statements suggest that you may *think* is your greatest need?

1. Look up each of the following Bible passages, discussing what each one says about your deepest needs:

   Mark 2:5, 9 _____

   Luke 7:47–48 _____

   Colossians 2:13 _____

   Do you agree that this is your deepest need? Why, or why not?

2. Recall a time when one of your children asked for forgiveness. What did you feel for your child?

   What could your feelings toward your child tell you about God's feelings toward you when you need forgiveness?

> *God pardons like a mother who kisses the offence into*
> *everlasting forgiveness.*
>
> HENRY WARD BEECHER,
> *PROVERBS FROM A PLYMOUTH PULPIT*

3. Describe an experience of forgiveness that has been life-changing for you or for someone you know personally.

Read Psalm 139 together. Have each person in your study read out loud a verse from this psalm, then discuss the following questions:

4. What does Psalm 139 suggest God knows about you? Be specific.

How does this intimate knowledge make you feel?

5. Discuss how the "shoulds" in your life (see the list in "For You Alone") can get in the way of trusting God with an intimate knowledge of who you really are.

6. What is your understanding of intimacy with God? What does it mean in day-to-day living?

7. Do you believe that greater intimacy with Jesus is the only antidote for guilt? If yes, state why. If no, state what could also be an effective antidote for guilt.

8. David, the man after God's own heart (Acts 13:22), was no stranger to failure, shame, disappointment, and sin. Yet he wasn't afraid to have God "search," "know," "test," and "see" him. Check out these verses, noting what David is confident of in each one:

Psalm 13:5 ————————————————————————

Psalm 18:19 ———————————————————————

Psalm 26:3 ————————————————————————

Psalm 27:13 ———————————————————————

Psalm 52:8–9 ———————————————————————

Psalm 56:3–4 ———————————————————————

For You and God

Once you cast off false guilt and trust God to search you, know you, test you, and see you in his perfect love, you can stop struggling and relax. Seeing yourself as God sees you will result in less shame and fear. The apostle John wrote, "There is no room in love for fear. Well-formed love banishes fear" (1 John 4:18 THE MESSAGE).

Find a quiet place. While there, confess your trust in God's love, and ask him to gently reveal and help you banish any false guilt. Then ask him to uncover any remaining ache in your soul—any true guilt. Here are two exercises that can help you lay yourself bare before God:

- Take out a piece of paper and write down everything you are holding against yourself in your mothering. Include past failures as well as current struggles. Be as specific as possible. Offer them to God for his forgiveness, and then either burn your list or tear it into tiny pieces, knowing that "He forgives your sins—every one" (Psalm 103:3 THE MESSAGE).

- Write about a shame-filled moment as a mother—yelling at your child, neglecting your child's needs, disregarding your child's feelings, being overcome by personal temptations and struggles, and so forth. Describe in detail every smell, sight, sound, and touch of this moment. Invite God into your story, asking for a sense of the fullness of his unconditional love and forgiveness. Then burn or tear up that piece of paper as a symbol of God's complete forgiveness.

For You and Your Kids

One of the wonderful by-products of intimacy with God is that you will be able to live humbly and authentically before your children, modeling to them the liberation of forgiveness. A study done several years ago reveals that the most influential interactions between parent and child are those where parents seek forgiveness from their children for their wrongdoings. Children who experience their parents asking for forgiveness develop confidence that they can take risks, make mistakes, and remain secure in relationships (see the book *Parenting by Heart* by Ron Taffel, with Melinda Blau [New York: Addison-Wesley, 1991]).

Preschool–Elementary

Do you remember pretending to be a mommy when you were a little girl? When your child pretends to be a mommy or a daddy, talk with her or him about the qualities of a parent that this pretend play reveals. Does their play or your conversation uncover ways in which you have failed your child? Take time to ask for forgiveness and to talk about ways you can better mother your children.

Middle–High School

Look together at the messages of your culture (magazines, movies, and advertisements)—what these messages say are your greatest needs. What does your culture suggest you need most? Wear certain brands? Have the right look? Acquire more stuff? Share with your children some of your own misconceptions about your deepest needs. Look for opportunities to remind your children that the deepest need of the human heart is to be fully known and forgiven by God.

All Ages

The message of God's story is that forgiveness is always available—you just have to ask. How can you translate God's message to your children? As you live in the fullness of God's forgiveness of your sin, you will be able to offer forgiveness to your children and at the same time point them to God. Don't miss the incredible opportunity that arises in the midst of failure—the opportunity of forgiveness. When you know you are forgiven—completely known and completely forgiven—you can mother without guilt.

> *Forgiveness is an answer, the divine answer, to the question implied in our existence. An answer is an answer only for him who has asked, who is aware of the question.*
>
> PAUL TILLICH,
> "TO WHOM MUCH WAS FORGIVEN"

if i'm forgiven,
why do i feel so bad?

> *In this way, love is made complete among us*
> *so that we will have confidence on the day of judgment,*
> *because in this world we are like him.*
> *There is no fear in love.*
> *But perfect love drives out fear,*
> *because fear has to do with punishment.*
> *The one who fears is not made perfect in love.*
>
> I JOHN 4:17–18

For You Alone

Get a stack of index cards. On each card write one thing you feel guilty about. List as many distinct guilty feelings as you can.

Now let's dissect your guilt. Begin by separating your "guilt cards" into two piles: "Things I can do something about" and "Things I can't do anything about." Set aside for a later time the stack of cards that you can do something about.

The remaining stack of cards is, for the most part, evidence of false guilt. These nagging feelings of guilt have to do with things you can't do anything about—things beyond your control. The cards in this stack probably fall into one of the following three categories:

- Disappointments
- Comparisons
- Resentments

Let's examine each to help you categorize and deal with your false guilt.

Disappointments

Read Proverbs 13:12. What experiences in your parenting have left your "heart sick"? Made you disappointed? Review the questions below to help you discover where and why you might be struggling with guilt produced by disappointment.

- Were you excited about the timing of your pregnancy or adoption?
- Did pregnancy and childbirth go as you anticipated it would?
- Was your newborn baby all you hoped he or she would be? Consider physical features, nursing experience, and other peoples' remarks.

> *Pregnancy and childbirth can be either heartbreaking or exhilarating. The same is true of the process of adoption. Whether these journeys go smoothly or not, there is no normative experience in our lives, apart from our own birth and death, that puts us through such massive change and transformation in such a relatively brief amount of time.*
>
> HARRIET LERNER, *THE MOTHER DANCE*

- Was your baby "easy" or "difficult" at church? At restaurants? On car trips?
- Did you like the way you looked during pregnancy, newborn days, toddler times?
- Did your child learn to walk, talk, tie shoes, recognize the alphabet, or learn to read like you hoped he or she would?
- Did you discover you had a hair-trigger temper once you became a mother?
- Did your child adjust to school easily?

- Did your child develop health problems?

- Does your child do well in school?

- Does your child have friends and get along well socially?

- Do you have a close relationship with your teenager?

- Is your adolescent moody, messy, or unreliable?

- Are you embarrassed by your teenager's appearance?

- Has your adolescent remained active and interested in church?

Look through your "guilt cards." Mark the ones that can be categorized as the result of disappointment.

Comparisons

Read 2 Corinthians 10:12. Comparisons entail quantifying and measuring one thing against another. It's tempting to compare our wardrobes, bodies, cars, housecleaning skills, and—yes—our children. Look at your "guilt cards" once again. How many are rooted in comparing your children or yourself with others? Identify the cards that are the result of comparing yourself with others and finding yourself coming up short.

> *When we don't accept people for who they are*
> *and try to change them, we usually end up*
> *in a snarled web of wasted energy.*
>
> STEVEN W. VANNOY,
> *THE GREATEST GIFTS OUR CHILDREN GIVE TO US*

Resentments

These are the poison of parenting. *Resentment* literally means "feeling again." Resentment goes over and over an old injury, misunderstanding, or disappointment. Resentment clings to anger and hurt. Look through your "guilt cards" once again. How many of these guilt feelings are associated with resentment over past hurts, failures, or disappointments? Now read Matthew 18:21–22. Have you ever said to yourself, "I will never put myself in a position to be hurt again"? Is your determination a result of resentments you are feeling over and over again? What does this passage suggest as the remedy for resentment?

For You and God's Word

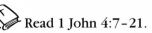 Read 1 John 4:7–21.

1. How does this passage describe "perfect love"?

2. How does false guilt keep you from loving in the manner described in 1 John 4? How is your false guilt translated into your mothering? If you suspect you may be laying guilt trips on your children, ask yourself, "What I am trying to achieve?" Are you motivated most by your own agenda or by what is best for your children?

3. Are you a "martyr mother"? Martyr moms harbor resentments and use guilt to keep their children close. Do you find yourself asking or saying—

    •   If you really loved me, you would . . .

    •   How can you act that way after all I've done for you?

    •   You never want to spend time with me.

    •   We never talk anymore.

What do you believe about yourself that results in your using guilt to motivate your children? Hint: look for traces of disappointment, comparison, or resentment.

> *Your own experience of God and his love is crucial because you will be able to translate only real-life experience to your [children] in parenting.*
>
> SHARON HERSH, *MOM, I FEEL FAT*

4. Go back and read again 1 John 4:17. What does this verse tell you about God's willingness to work within you to eliminate false guilt forever?

The amazing process of give-and-take in your understanding of God's love will allow you to confront your disappointments, comparisons, and resentments—all those feelings that can produce false guilt in your life—and release them to a God who loves perfectly. His forgiveness, support, grace, guidance, mercy, and unshakable commitment to you can banish guilt.

No one has seen God, ever. But if we love one another,
God dwells deeply within us, and His love becomes
complete in us—perfect love!

1 JOHN 4:12 THE MESSAGE

Take each "guilt card" and confess the disappointment, comparison, or resentment to God. Then cut up each card and discard it. Say good-bye to useless guilt.

For You and Others

1. With your small group discuss some favorite "motherisms" and how they may be rooted in false guilt, remembering the disappointments, comparisons, and resentments that produce such guilt. Here are a few to get you started. Be sure to add others that come to mind.

    *   I can't stop worrying until you get home.

    *   Do as I say, not as I do.

    *   I would never have talked to my mother like that.

    *   What will people think?

    *   This hurts me more than it hurts you.

    *   Your action is a reflection on our entire family.

    *   Why can't you do this for me?

    Read together as a group 1 John 4:7–21.

2. How does verse 9 suggest that the love of God is made visible?

3. How do verses 16 and 19 suggest that we can make our love for God visible to others?

4. When you struggle with guilt, what does verse 16 suggest you are to rely on?

Read Psalm 22:5.

5. What does this verse tell you about God's love for people who struggle with disappointment? Who is the only one who will never disappoint?

6. Why do you think people still trust in other things and then are surprised when disappointment comes?

Read Philippians 2:5–8.

7. Who is being compared with whom in this passage?

8. What does this passage reveal about comparisons and about how God demonstrates his love for you?

Read Romans 3:22–24.

9. How does God's love respond to your repeated failures? Concentrate on the word *freely* in verse 24. (You may want to highlight, underline, and circle this wonderful word in your Bible.)

How is his response different from your own response to your repeated failures? Are you harsher with yourself than God is with you? Why?

10. If God's love is the model to imitate, you need to know—deep in your heart and soul—how God loves you. Recall a time when you truly experienced God's love.

Now, as a group turn to Isaiah 43:25.

11. What does God promise? What do you think is meant by "blots out"? What does God mean when he says he won't remember your sins? Why, then, should you remember them?

Finally, turn to Isaiah's mesmerizing words in Isaiah 43:18-19.

12. What "former things" should you forget? What things about your past should you no longer dwell on?

13. What effect would taking the words of Isaiah to heart have on your feelings of guilt? On your effectiveness as a mother?

14. What "new thing" is God willing to do in your life? Are you ready for him to do it?

For You and God

If you give up the belief that your children are your report card, you can begin to see them as God intended you to — his perfect gift to you (James 1:17). Your children *are* a gift. In unrestricted, unconditional love, God gave you your children. Can you believe that *you* are the mother God wanted your children to have?

When you look at your children, instead of seeing disappointment, can you see God's wisdom in *entrusting them to you?* Jot down on a piece of paper what you see as your unique gifts and personality traits that can bless your children.

When you look at your children, instead of comparing them with others, can you see them uniquely as *God's gift to you?* Reflect for a few moments on how their struggles, accomplishments, and individual personality traits have been gifts to you.

When you look at your children, instead of rehearsing old wounds and hurtful situations over and over again, can you envision all that God is doing in you and then in and through your relationship with your children?

In prayer, thank God for his gift of your children. Then ask him to help you form a faith-filled vision for a relationship that encompasses not only the unique individual you are as their mom but also the unique individuals your children are.

For You and Your Kids

Now it's time to pick up the stack of "guilt cards" that represent things you *can* do something about. How can you take action against each guilt? For example, you may need to tell your child you are sorry for holding on to resentment about a particular failure or mistake. Apologizing will release you from guilt and empower you to see your children as gifts.

Preschool–Elementary

Keep a journal of all the funny and quirky things your children do and say. Read through the journal together, using the stories to tell your children what you know to be true of them. Spending this time together will remind you and your children of what is really true about you and them — and it will help to combat false guilt when it rears its ugly head in the form of disappointments, comparisons, or resentments.

Middle–High School

Has there ever been an occasion when you knew your son or daughter needed you or was in trouble, even though he or she couldn't or didn't tell you about it? Have you awakened in the middle of the night and known you needed to pray about something with regard to your child? Tell your child about this mysterious connection and its confirmation that *you* are God's choice as the best mother for your child.

All Ages

False guilt, fueled by disappointments, comparisons, and resentments, can keep you from being a mom of power and conviction. However, when you experience—heart and soul—God's love for you, you can love your children powerfully and effectively. When you are free from the grip of false guilt, you will have more energy to love. There is no more compelling motivation to say "good-bye" to guilt!

> *First we were loved, now we love.*
>
> I JOHN 4:19 THE MESSAGE

mentors in mothering: jochebed — let go

> *[Jochebed] became pregnant and give birth to a son.*
> *When she saw that he was a fine child,*
> *she hid him for three months.*
> *But when she could hide him no longer,*
> *she got a papyrus basket for him*
> *and coated it with tar and pitch.*
> *Then she placed the child in it and put it*
> *among the reeds along the bank of the Nile.*
>
> EXODUS 2:2–3

For You Alone

Jochebed was a mother during uncertain and dangerous times. When the midwife announced, "It's a boy!" Jochebed knew that her son had been born into a world where the very law of the land put him in grave peril. Pharaoh had decreed, "Every boy that is born you must throw into the Nile" (Exodus 1:22). Certainly, Pharaoh's words rang in Jochebed's ears and pierced her heart as she held her newborn son.

What images, threats, hopes, and fears stirred in your heart as you brought your children into this world? Circle the words that best describe your persistent thoughts, fears, and hopes regarding your children and their future:

Violence	Success	Depression	Addiction
Affluence	Good health	Divorce	Intelligence
Sadness	Athleticism	Humor	Loneliness
War	Terrorism	Friendship	Spiritual growth
Rebellion	Failure	Happiness	Compliance
Popularity	Leadership	Shyness	Poverty
Sickness	Sexual abuse	Friendliness	Happiness

Look back at each circled word and answer the following questions:

- Do I worry about this for my child because of my own experience? Because of current events?

- Do I want this for my child because I never experienced this myself? Because I know this will bring him or her a better future?

- Do I believe I am responsible to prevent this reality or make this a reality for my child?

- Based on your reflections and answers above, what are you holding on most tightly to: to the past, to control of current events, or to responsibility for future outcomes?

*Unless a sense of wonder accompanies parenthood,
we may either take our responsibility too lightly
or else cling too tightly to our children.*

JEAN FLEMING, *A MOTHER'S HEART*

For You and God's Word

Read Exodus 1:1–2:8. Answer the following questions as though you are Moses' mother, Jochebed:

1. What does your people's past (Exodus 1:8–14) predict about their future?

2. What emotions and fears do these current events provoke (Exodus 1:15–22)?

3. What is the most likely future for your son (Exodus 2:1–8)?

Try to imagine all that was stirring in Jochebed's heart as she hid her infant son from enemy hands and then *released* him into the hands of the very same enemy. Only a mother can read this story and fully appreciate Jochebed's fear and pain and humility and trust as she surrendered her son to Pharaoh's daughter. Mothers can smile with Jochebed as she creatively invited Pharaoh's daughter to allow her to nurse her own son. Try to picture what Jochebed might have said to Moses as she fed him and prepared him to leave her. What might have soothed her heart during this strange and sorrowful mothering season?

You can answer these questions by examining the words of Moses as a grown man—words he no doubt learned from his mother:

> Hear, O Israel: The LORD our God, the LORD is one.
> Love the LORD your God with all your heart
> and with all your soul and with all your strength.
> These commandments that I give you today are to be
> upon your hearts. Impress them on your children.
> Talk about them when you sit at home and when you
> walk along the road, when you lie down
> and when you get up.
>
> DEUTERONOMY 6:4–7

4. Read Deuteronomy 7:7–9 and jot down what this passage suggests Moses believed about God and his past dealings with his people.

Read Deuteronomy 10:12–22 and jot down what Moses believed about God in the midst of current events.

Read Deuteronomy 11:22–25 and jot down what Moses believed about the future.

The past, the present, and the future all urge us to be at war with each other, with God, and with ourselves. We can find ample evidence to support the following sentiments:

- Be resentful about the past.
- Be anxious about the future.
- Be dissatisfied with what you see.
- Feel guilty.
- Be in control.

Certainly, Jochebed could have easily been ruled by any and all of these sentiments. But instead, *she chose to let go.*

For You and Others

Read Exodus 1:15–17.

1. Imagine the Israelite midwives and women of childbearing age getting together during this time. Imagine Jochebed among them during her pregnancy. Discuss together what you think they may have talked about. Describe the emotions and reactions you would have had if you had been there. These emotions and reactions set the stage for all that the midwives and Jochebed decided to do.

Read Exodus 1:1–7.

2. What does this passage suggest the Israelites, including the mothers, remembered from their past?

3. During dangerous and uncertain times, what do you remember from your past? What do you remember about your parents? About your failures and successes? About God's fingerprints in your life?

4. How can memories of the past affect how you mother your children? Include both negative influences and positive influences.

Review Exodus 1:8–22.

5. Describe the "current events" of Jochebed's day.

6. Look through a current-events magazine *(Time, Newsweek, U.S. News & World Report)*. Discuss what sorts of events provoke fear, especially for mothers. How do current events influence your mothering?

Read Exodus 2:1–10.

7. What does this passage hint about Jochebed's longings for her son and his future?

8. As you ponder the future for each of your children, discuss what you as mothers long for. Consider several areas of life—educational, emotional, physical, spiritual, marital, and so forth. How do these longings affect your mothering?

Read Hebrews 11:23.

9. What does this passage tell you about Jochebed and what made "letting go" possible for her?

10. As a group discuss times of "letting go" in mothering. Perhaps it was when you first left your baby in the nursery at church, when you returned to work after your baby's birth, your child's first day of school, or the first time your teenager took the car out alone. What made "letting go" possible?

How did letting go change your perspective of mothering?

How does your personal relationship with God affect your ability to let go of your children?

For You and God

Nothing stirs your mother's heart and longings quite like your children. You long for them to be happy, successful, and good. It's easy to get confused about what is your part and what is God's part. When you take responsibility for what you can't or shouldn't control, letting go of your children becomes practically impossible.

In your time alone with God today, consider these words:

> *Those who think they can [make it] on their own become obsessed with measuring their own moral muscle but never get around to exercising it in real life. Those who trust God's action in them find that God's Spirit is in them—living and breathing God! Obsession with self in these matters is a dead end; attention to God leads us out into the open, into a spacious, free life. Focusing on the self is the opposite of focusing on God. Anyone completely absorbed in self ignores God, ends up thinking more about self than God.*
>
> ROMANS 8:5–8 THE MESSAGE

In the midst of dangerous and confusing current events, what do you hold on to as a mother? Do you hold on to God? Or do you hold on to self?

Consider the words of nineteenth-century pastor Henry Venn to a mother whose son had a greater appetite for pleasure than for God: "[This painful experience should teach you about] your own weakness and inability to give a single ray of light, or to excite the faintest conviction of sin, or to communicate the least particle of spiritual good, to one who is dearer to you than life. How ought this to take away every proud thought of our own sufficiency, and to keep us earnest, importunate supplicants at the door of the Almighty's mercy and free grace." What does this say to *you* about letting go?

What do you have to let go of in order to face the future with courage and creativity? Ask God to work in you so that you are absorbed with him rather than with trying to control the events of your life and your children's lives on your own.

For You and Your Kids

Your creativity in mothering is released when you let go of hurts, fears, and failures, as you are rooted in the unshakable faith that God can be trusted. In turn, your children's faith is born and creativity is fueled as they see you live in light of the truth that nothing in your past, present, or future can keep God's steadfast love from reaching you.

Preschool–Elementary

Use a flashlight to illustrate faith in God. Remove the batteries, and have your young children try to turn the flashlight on. Then put fresh batteries inside and turn it on. Light! Explain that the batteries are like God within them. When they trust God's care for them, their faith works like the batteries, and they have light to see where they've been and where they're going. Encourage your young children to remember that God is within them when they face both wonderful pleasures (a good grade, winning a game, a fun evening at home) and heartbreaking losses (friends who hurt their feelings, the loss of a grandparent, natural disasters).

To help them understand God within them, link the "experiencing" of God with their feelings of love. Ask, "How much do you love me?" Explain that God loves them even more. Children *know* God; they just don't have the vocabulary to express their knowing.

Middle–High School

Celebrate the occasions when you "let go" of your older children. Mark the times of transition and greater independence for your child by praying together, giving your child something symbolic of the occasion (a "purity" ring before a first date, for instance), and reminding your child (and yourself) that you are letting go, trusting your child more, and entrusting him or her into God's care.

All Ages

You can let go of your children only to the degree that you trust in God. During dangerous and confusing times, you know Someone who is steadfast and wise, who encircles them and you with arms of love and who will never let go. The familiar motto "Let go and let God" can be a good reminder for moms who long to mother without fear and guilt and with grace and confidence.

> *If someone were to ask you, "What is the one thing in life that is certain?" you would have to answer, "The love of Christ." Not parents, not family, not friends. Not art or science or philosophy or any of the products of human wisdom. Only the love of Christ.*
>
> BRENNAN MANNING, *RUTHLESS TRUST*

mentors in mothering: deborah — take heart

> Village life in Israel ceased,
>
>   ceased until I, Deborah, arose,
>
>   arose a mother in Israel.
>
> JUDGES 5:7

For You Alone

The Canaanites swept over Israel — rampaging, killing, and pillaging — until the natural order of village life ceased to exist (Judges 5:7). Because the people of Israel forgot their faith and "did evil in the eyes of the LORD" (Judges 3:7), God sent the Canaanites to punish them. During these darkest of times, Deborah arrived on the scene. Deborah challenged the Israelites to remember God and return to their faith. In fact, her influence turned the course of an entire nation. What gave her the wisdom and courage to lead during this difficult time? Her mother's heart (Judges 5:7). In this session you will look at the divinely implanted mother's heart and consider how understanding your heart for your children can not only overcome guilt, but also lead you in becoming a powerful influence.

Circle the most accurate response to each statement.

1. I am confident as I face questions and decisions in mothering.

    Often   Sometimes   Rarely   Never

2. I enjoy playing and having fun with my children.

    Often   Sometimes   Rarely   Never

3. I am concerned about the spiritual lives of my children.

    Often   Sometimes   Rarely   Never

4. I do what needs to be done for my children, even if it's scary.

    Often   Sometimes   Rarely   Never

5. I am not afraid to try new things with my children.

    Often   Sometimes   Rarely   Never

6. I am flooded with love for my children.

    Often   Sometimes   Rarely   Never

7. I have creative ideas for mothering my children.

    Often   Sometimes   Rarely   Never

8. I am excited about mothering.

    Often   Sometimes   Rarely   Never

9. My children seem to enjoy being around me.

   Often   Sometimes   Rarely   Never

10. I use my imagination in mothering.

    Often   Sometimes   Rarely   Never

11. I spend time in solitude, which rejuvenates me for mothering.

    Often   Sometimes   Rarely   Never

12. I am overwhelmed with gratitude for my children.

    Often   Sometimes   Rarely   Never

13. I am overwhelmed with gratitude for the privilege of mothering.

    Often   Sometimes   Rarely   Never

14. I believe I am a good mother.

    Often   Sometimes   Rarely   Never

15. I have fun mothering.

    Often   Sometimes   Rarely   Never

16. Mothering feels like a great adventure.

    Often   Sometimes   Rarely   Never

17.   I feel an alliance with God as I mother.

Often   Sometimes   Rarely   Never

18.   I welcome the challenges of mothering.

Often   Sometimes   Rarely   Never

19.   I believe mothering is the most important "work" in the kingdom.

Often   Sometimes   Rarely   Never

20.   I know that I am the best mother for my children.

Often   Sometimes   Rarely   Never

The scoring for this little questionnaire is simple. If you didn't answer "Often" to *every one* of the questions, you are not as fully connected to your "mother's heart" as you can be and as God intends you be.

Perhaps you're thinking, *Any mom who says she feels all these things* often *is pretty arrogant and not in touch with reality.*

But is that really true? Remember—we're not saying *always.* Just *often.*

Look through the questionnaire again. What do you think you *shouldn't* feel? How much are your answers influenced by guilt? The good news is that God designed you with a mother's heart, and when you are connected to his design and purposes for you, you will feel confidence, gratitude, love, playfulness, and creativity. And you will experience a deeper connection to God *and* your children!

> *Hand-in-hand mothering begins with a fervent belief*
> *that you are the right mother for your daughter,*
> *that God has implanted in you the seeds of longing*
> *for relationship that can bloom into an empowering*
> *alliance between you and your child.*
>
> SHARON HERSH, *MOM, I FEEL FAT!*

For You and God's Word

Read the moving story of two moms in 1 Kings 3:16–27.

1. What does this passage suggest about a mother's innate longing and wisdom with regard to her children?

2. How could trusting your own intuition and knowing your children intimately diminish feelings of guilt? What keeps you from this sort of confidence in mothering?

Read the song of Deborah in Judges 5.

3. What clues to Deborah's confidence as a "mother in Israel" can you find in verses 2–3? Verse 9? Verse 11?

4. What confidence can you gain as a mother from verse 31?

5. What or who has the greatest influence on your children? What keeps you from believing you are the most significant influence?

6. How could believing that you are the most powerful influence in your children's lives combat feelings of guilt?

7. Recall a time when you had to make a difficult parenting decision. What did you rely on?

What keeps you from relying on your own love and longing for your child?

8. How could an alliance with God increase your confidence?

A study by Teenage Research Unlimited found that
70 percent of teenagers name their mom or dad
as the person they most admire.

JUDY FORD AND AMANDA FORD,
BETWEEN MOTHER & DAUGHTER

For You and Others

Begin your time as a small group by reading Judges 4 and 5 together.

1. Describe the "mood" of Deborah's day. Look for specifics.

2. How was Deborah's time like yours? Different from yours?

3. What was Deborah's "job description"? (See Judges 4:4-7.)

4. During these difficult and dangerous days, what does Deborah call herself (Judges 5:7)? How is that significant?

5. What does Judges 4:4-5 tell you about Deborah?

6. Write your own definition for wisdom, including in it specifics for mothering.

7. What quality is evident in Deborah's instructions to Barak in Judges 4:6, 14?

8. Write your own definition for influence, highlighting the influence a mother has.

9. Read Hebrews 11:32–33. How does Deborah's influence show up in this chapter about men and women of great faith?

10. Years from now, what sort of influence might your children recall that you had on them? What sort of influence do you hope they recall? What actions can you take to be sure this happens?

11. Israel's enemy had _____,

    was _____, and had oppressed them for

    _____ years (Judges 4:3).

12. Who is your enemy (see 1 Peter 5:8)? What is he like?

13. In the face of her enemy, what quality is communicated in Deborah's decision and words in Judges 4:8-9?

14. Write your definition of courage for mothers.

15. What characteristic does Deborah demonstrate when faced with the enemy (Judges 4:14)?

16. Write a personal definition of faith. Make it specific to your mothering.

17. Deborah led ten thousand men (Judges 4:10) and was not intimidated by the task at hand or by those around her. What or who intimidates you in mothering? How does or should your faith respond to these feelings of intimidation?

18. What was the source of Deborah's faith and strength (Judges 5:2, 5, 9)?

19. Describe an event or circumstance in mothering that requires faith. Where can you find the faith to act with confidence in this circumstance?

20. What happens to guilt when faith becomes fully involved in your mothering? How does a lack of faith affect guilt in your mothering?

21. Judges 5 is often referred to as "Deborah's Song of Remembrance." What does Deborah remember? Why was it important for Deborah and Israel to remember these events?

22. Remember a specific season or significant event in your mothering. Recall specific sounds, tastes, smells, and sensations of touch. Why is remembering important for you and your family?

23. What does Judges 3:7 say about the importance of remembering?

> *Sorrow cannot steal our faith or even cause it to be lost; betrayal and loss steal our faith only when we refuse to remember, tell our stories, listen even as we tell them, and explore the meaning that God has woven into them. If we want to grow in faith, we must be open to listening to our own stories, perhaps familiar or forgotten, where we have not mined the rich deposit of God's presence.*
>
> DAN ALLENDER, *THE HEALING PATH*

For You and God

Wisdom, influence, courage, faith, and remembering characterized Deborah's mother heart. This section (as well as "For You and Your Kids") includes exercises to help you develop each of these areas of *your* mother heart.

Wisdom

What do you rely on when you make mothering decisions? Check all that apply:

- ❑ your own experience
- ❑ parenting experts
- ❑ friends and family
- ❑ faith in and reliance on God and his leading
- ❑ your own intuition
- ❑ your understanding of your child

The best mothering involves a combination of all six components listed above. Where are you lacking? Below are some questions to help you with each area:

- If you could repeat a part of your childhood, which part would it be? Why? If you could change a part of your past, which part would it be? Why? How can your answers inform your parenting decisions today?

- When was the last time you read a parenting book? Read a new book, or reread an old favorite. This time, as you read, note what the book brings to mind about your mothering strengths.

- When was the last time you affirmed one of your friends in her mothering? Call a friend today and commit to helping her see her unique gifts and strengths in parenting.

- Do you pray about daily decisions in parenting? Pick a time (while making breakfast, waiting in the checkout lane, doing the dishes) to pray specifically about mothering matters.

- Write down qualities and characteristics that you value about yourself. How often do you let these influence your parenting decisions?

- Commit to spending time alone with each of your kids on a regular basis in order to get to know and understand them better.

Remembering

Separate your life into decades. Pull out old photographs to help you remember. As you review each decade, consider writing a "Song of Remembrance." The following prompts might help you in your recollections:

- The most significant event during this time was . . .
- This event affected my life in the following ways . . .
- The person(s) who influenced me most was (were) . . .
- The life lesson from this season of my life was . . .
- I can see God's fingerprints on . . .

Faith

Read Romans 10:17. Are you relying on this source of faith? Read some of the Bible's stories of mothering, asking God to strengthen your faith through them. Consider Sarah's fierce protection of her son (Genesis 21:1–21), Jochebed's creativity and courage in caring for Moses (Exodus 2:1–10), Ruth and Naomi's joy in Obed (Ruth 4:13–17), Hannah's selfless surrender of her son (1 Samuel 1:1–18; 2:18–21), and, of course, Mary—Jesus' mother— pondering in her heart all that was happening and then weeping at his feet as he died (Luke 2; John 19:25–27).

For You and Your Kids

Influence: Preschool–Elementary

Devise a "Getting to Know You" quiz to take periodically with your children. Go out for lunch or for a picnic in the park, then take the quiz together to see how well you know each other. Your most powerful influence is released when your children feel that you're connected to them. Here are some questions you could include on the quiz:

- If you had lots of money, what would you buy?
- What's your favorite song right now?

- What's the best way for you to snap out of a bad mood?
- What are five things you like about yourself?

Influence: Middle–High School

Do you pray for your children's culture? Parents often spend a lot of time criticizing or combating the culture, only to find that their children have embraced the culture. Consider praying every day that God's presence will influence some aspect of your child's culture. Share quietly and quickly—don't overdo this or you just might drive your teens away—that they and their culture are in your daily prayers.

Courage: All Ages

Most people tend to think of courage in connection with big events and larger-than-life undertakings. But courage is really more a matter of the heart and of day-to-day living—facing whatever life brings, investing in the lives of others.

Is there a cause or an organization that you and your children can become involved in? This could be a rescue mission, a shelter for battered women, or a mission organization. It takes initiative and courage to invest in the lives of others, but the payoff to you and your children is guaranteed (see Galatians 6:9). Guilt is often the result of self-absorption as we obsess about our mishaps and mistakes. One antidote for guilt is a courageous involvement with others.

mentors in mothering: mary — have faith

> *Blessed is she who has believed that what the Lord has said to her will be accomplished!*
>
> LUKE 1:45

For You Alone

Using a big sheet of paper and lots of crayons, draw a "road map" of your spiritual life. Think about it first, perhaps reviewing your recollections about your life from previous sessions in this study. A road map of your spiritual life is not about your journey to a specific accomplishment (job, college degree, marriage, and so forth). To draw a map of your spiritual journey is to look for experiences and transitions, triumphs and struggles, turning points and times of waiting that have contributed to making you the person you are. Your road map may include some external milestones (like college graduation or parenthood), but it should also include references to your internal life (like a time of reflection, a season of melancholy, or a burst of creativity). There is no wrong or right way to complete this exercise. When you're finished, you'll see an accumulation of doubt and certainty, understanding and accomplishment, and personal and professional battlefields. (Fold up your road map and place it in your study guide, ready to bring along to share with others during the "For You and Others" time.)

After completing your road map, read what Henri Nouwen wrote in *Reaching Out:*

> What if the events of our history are molding us as a sculptor molds his clay, and if it is only in a careful obedience to these molding hands that we can discover our real vocation and become mature people? What if all the unexpected interruptions are in fact invitations to give up old-fashioned and outmoded styles of living and are opening up new unexplored areas of experience? And finally: What if our history does not prove to be a blind, impersonal sequence of events over which we have no control, but rather reveals to us a guiding hand pointing to a personal encounter in which all our hopes and aspirations will reach their fulfillment? Then our life would indeed be different, because then fate becomes opportunity, wounds a warning, and paralysis an invitation to search for deeper sources of vitality.

Spend some time considering these questions:

- Where do you see God's guiding hand on your road map?

- What hopes and aspirations have reached their fulfillment in your journey? Did they reach their fulfillment the way you thought they would?

- Recall interruptions in your life path. What opportunities have these interruptions brought to you?

- How have the difficult and disappointing times directed your spiritual journey?

- How has pain and sorrow changed the course of your journey?

- Where does guilt stake its claims along the way?

- As you look at your road map, what surprises you?

For You and God's Word

Read Luke 1:26–45 and Luke 2:1–52. Mary became a mother under the most unusual and trying circumstances. Young, unmarried, and without many resources, she learned from an angel that she was going to have a baby. Her faith was conceived in the inconceivable. The song that burst from her lips—the *Magnificat*—tells you something of Mary's faith. Even though her position was humble and her circumstances considered suspect by many, Mary's faith banished shame, doubt, and false guilt. Her faith was made visible during the unfolding life of her son, and her faith was complete in his finished work. In this session you'll look at Mary's story and her unshakable faith in God's promise. You will be encouraged that God's promise is at work in your life, too.

1. Put yourself in the story. Describe all that may have transpired in Mary's heart and mind between verses 26 and 38 of Luke 1.

Mary reached the place of surrender in verse 38, in part, because she knew that God had given her a special child—a child of promise and purpose (Luke 1:30–33).

2. Recall when you learned that you were pregnant. Did you have a sense of God's promise and purpose during your pregnancy? Why? Why not? Sometimes faith looks forward; other times it looks backward. Looking back, can you see God's promise and purpose in the birth of your child?

Mary's faith was tested right from the start. Consider Mary's journey to Bethlehem when she was nine months pregnant. She must have questioned the census—why now of all times! She couldn't help but feel the discomfort of their journey and inconvenience of their leftover lodgings. The events of Jesus' birth and early life were exciting, yet undoubtedly unsettling, for Mary.

3. Given all of these experiences, what do you think Mary "treasured" and "pondered" (Luke 2:19, 51)?

4. What unexplainable or unpleasant circumstances have been a part of your mothering experience? Can you see them as part of God's design for you and your child?

> *Maybe we simply need to realize that our most unpleasant circumstances, much like Mary's and Joseph's, often have a way of becoming a beautiful portion of God's magnificent design.*
>
> JONI EARECKSON TADA, *A CHRISTMAS LONGING*

For You and Others

Read Luke 1:26–45 and Luke 2:1–52 together as a group. If you have someone in your group who is gifted in dramatic reading, have her read the story out loud to everyone.

1. List the unexpected and unexplainable events in Mary's life described in these passages.

2. Sometime during her pregnancy, Mary went to visit her cousin Elizabeth (Luke 1:39–45). How far apart were they in age (compare Luke 1:7 and 1:27)? How do you think the age difference may have affected their friendship?

3. How did Elizabeth encourage Mary? What do you think this visit may have accomplished for Mary?

4. How have friendships with other mothers affected you as you mother your children? As you deal with difficult events in your life?

5. Based on your study of Mary's life so far, share together what you think she "treasured" and "pondered" in her heart (Luke 2:19, 51).

6. Together draw a "spiritual road map" of Mary's life, based on the emotions and reactions suggested in the following passages:

Luke 1:29_____

Luke 1:30_____

Luke 1:34_____

Luke 1:38_____

Luke 2:6_____

Luke 2:19_____

Luke 2:33 _____

Luke 2:35 _____

Luke 2:48 _____

Luke 2:50 _____

Luke 2:51 _____

7. Form groups of two or three. Share your own personal spiritual road maps with each other. Point out your highs and lows, your victories and defeats. Answer any questions the others may have about your map. You will inevitably learn more about your own journey as you describe it to others and also as you look at and hear about theirs.

8. How does sharing your experiences with others increase or diminish any guilt with which you are struggling? How could this small group help you deal with and gain victory over any lingering feelings of guilt?

> *Disclosure is powerful, both for the speaker and the listener. Often, it is in telling another the truth about ourselves that we discover the truth more fully. Sixteenth-century poet John of the Cross warns about the consequences of not being transparent: "The virtuous soul that is alone and without witnesses is like a burning coal. It will grow colder rather than hotter."*
>
> SHARON HERSH, *BRAVEHEARTS*

For You and God

Get out your spiritual road map again. Review the times you struggled with defeat or pain or felt that God was absent. While looking at your map, ask yourself what happens to guilt when you view the difficult times in your life through the lens of God's promise and purpose. Have you tended to view inconvenience, discomfort, or hardship as evidence that something "went wrong" in your life? How does Mary's story contradict this view?

Consider that Mary—unmarried, a virgin—learned from an angel that she was pregnant. She gave birth in a cave, far away from home. In astonishment and anxiety she watched her son grow (Luke 2:48) and mourned his death at the foot of a cross. Yet the angel of the Lord told Mary that she was "highly favored" (Luke 1:28). Is it possible that the heartaches and hardships of your own mothering experience show God's favor of you? How?

Using the trusty crayons again, draw a large cross over your entire road map. Sometimes the only evidence of God's goodness is the cross, and sometimes the only evidence of God's power is the resurrection. But what goodness and power that is! Read and memorize 1 Corinthians 15:57, using it to frame a prayer to God as you ask him to give you his perspective on the dark areas of your life and as you praise him for the victories you've experienced.

For You and Your Kids

Preschool–Elementary

Children are naturally drawn to nature, and God's creation is a wonderful means to see the hand of the Creator and his purpose and promise for his creatures. Faith is born in moments of noting God's presence in the details of a robin's egg, the perfectly formed spider's web, the birth of a new puppy, the loving action of a mother bird as she feeds her babies, and the smell of the earth after a rain shower. Have fun with this concept. Consider God's purpose for mosquitoes, a winter blizzard, or a hairy head. Read and talk about God's promise in Matthew 6:26: "Look at the birds, free and unfettered, not tied down to a job description, careless in the care of God. And you count far more to him than birds" (THE MESSAGE).

Middle–High School

Share your road map with your children. Encourage them to draw their own spiritual journeys. Look together for God's fingerprints along the way.

All Ages

Awaken your children before sunrise one morning and tell them you're taking them on an adventure. Pack a thermos filled with hot chocolate and some favorite breakfast snacks. Walk (with flashlights in hand) or drive to a spot to watch the sunrise. Share with your children the faithfulness of God in the newness of each day. You might want to plan this "sunrise surprise" right before the start of a new school year or during a discouraging time as a reminder that the sunrise is daily evidence of God's promise that he is with them.

> Yet this I call to mind
>   and therefore I have hope:
> Because of the LORD's great love we are not consumed,
>   for his compassions never fail.
> They are new every morning;
>   great is your faithfulness.
> I say to myself, "The LORD is my portion;
>   therefore I will wait for him."
>
> LAMENTATIONS 3:21–24

mentors in mothering: lois and eunice — be an example

I have been reminded of your sincere faith, which first lived in your grandmother Lois and in your mother Eunice and, I am persuaded, now lives in you also.

2 TIMOTHY 1:5

For You Alone

Think of someone who has been a mentor to you as a mother. Perhaps it's your mom or a sister or a friend or an older woman at church. Record here this person's character qualities and unique personality quirks, as well as the ways in which she has helped and encouraged you. Write down what specifically she has modeled for you. The following questions can guide you in developing your thoughts further.

- When you were younger, whom did you want to be like? Why?

- List your childhood heroes. What qualities do they share?

- When did you first have to take a stand of some sort as an adolescent? Who encouraged you?

- Recall a time of hurt or confusion. Who spoke encouraging words to you at that time?

- When has someone believed in you? How did his or her beliefs influence you?

- Who has noticed your unique gifts and abilities and encouraged them?

- Who made you feel like they wanted to be with you?

- Who encouraged you to dream?

- Finish this sentence: I would not be who I am today if it

  were not for _____.

> *These are my roots that daily name me and help me discover more of who I am ... my father, my grandmother, my great-grandfather, my friends, my counselors.*

For You and God's Word

The "sincere faith" of Timothy's mother and grandmother replicated in Timothy an authentic faith as well (2 Timothy 1:5). Lois and Eunice instilled in Timothy a love and respect for the Scriptures (2 Timothy 3:14–15) and planted in his heart a desire to minister to others (Acts 16:1–3).

After reading these passages, fill in your conclusions about Lois and Eunice and their hearts for Timothy:

- Lois and Eunice were more interested in _____ than external appearances.

- Lois and Eunice thought more about eternal life than _____.

- Timothy's mother and grandmother must have talked often about a relationship with _____.

- Lois and Eunice used the _____ to teach Timothy.

- Timothy's mother and grandmother taught him that living a _____ (2 Timothy 1:9) was more important than any sort of personal comfort or gain.

Review the five statements. Circle those that already describe your mothering. Underline those you need to work on as a mother. Now write three statements that you long for your children to be able to ~~say about you when they are grown:~~

1. ——————————————————————

2.

3.

Where can you find the power to begin (see 2 Thessalonians 2:16–17)?

For You and Others

The apostle Paul commended Timothy for his walk with God and acknowledged what Timothy had earned from the lives of his mother and grandmother. Read the following passages together, noting what they tell you about Timothy's faith and his mother's and grandmother's influence:

1. What does Acts 16:1–5 tell you about Timothy's family?

2. Who doesn't participate in Timothy's spiritual life? How might this be an encouragement to some of you?

3. What trait does the apostle Paul trace from Timothy to his mother and grandmother (2 Timothy 1:5)?

Write your own definition for *sincere faith.*

Read 2 Timothy 1:1–14 together.

4. Jot down what the apostle Paul describes as attributes of a sincere faith.

5. In 1 Timothy 1:18–19 Paul mentions prophecies made about Timothy. What do you think these prophecies said about Timothy? How could these prophecies have affected what his mother and grandmother thought about him?

6. What character traits are evident in Timothy's life (2 Timothy 1:17)? How could these attributes be translated into your mothering?

7. What does 1 Timothy 4:12 suggest is unusual about Timothy's faith?

8. What does Paul tell Timothy he should be (1 Timothy 4:12)?

That precious memory triggers another: your honest faith—and what a rich faith it is, handed down from your grandmother Lois to your mother Eunice, and now to you!

2 TIMOTHY 1:5 THE MESSAGE

9. According to the following verses, what does Paul mean when he tells Timothy to be an example to others?

1 Timothy 4:13 _____

1 Timothy 4:14 _____

1 Timothy 4:15 _____

1 Timothy 4:16 _____

1 Timothy 6:20 _____

2 Timothy 2:22 _____

2 Timothy 2:23 _____

2 Timothy 2:24 _____

2 Timothy 2:25

How can each of these actions and attributes be applied to your daily life and activity as a mother?

10. What played an important role in Timothy's mother's and grandmother's influence (2 Timothy 3:14–15)? How can this also play a significant role in your life as a mother? In your children's lives?

Timothy's life of faith did not begin in a vacuum. God pointedly reveals the powerful influence of Timothy's mother and grandmother. If you read the passages about Timothy with an open heart, you'll see what changed his life—and can change yours and can change the people you love. The encouragement to be found in the story of Timothy is that Timothy's mother and grandmother powerfully influenced his life by their real faith—not by their perfect homes, beautiful wardrobes, or many accomplishments, but by their real faith.

11. Share ways that you try to make your faith real to your children. Listen and learn from other mothers in your group. Discuss concrete ideas for translating your faith into daily experiences with your children.

12. Talk about how you got to where you are today in your relationship with God and the importance of others' influence. If you feel comfortable, share something of what you recorded about your mentor in "For You Alone."

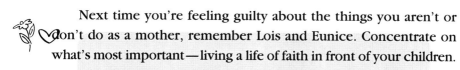

Next time you're feeling guilty about the things you aren't or don't do as a mother, remember Lois and Eunice. Concentrate on what's most important—living a life of faith in front of your children.

For You and God

The mentor, then, looks two ways—backward and
forward—asking "Who am I?" and "Where am I going?"

DON HUDSON, "THE THREE LANGUAGES OF MENTORING"

In your time with God, reflect on what your relationship with the mentor you introduced at the beginning of this session has taught you about yourself. Identify your unique talents and authentic gifts, and jot down ways in which you're using them in mothering.

Make a list of the positive things you have to give to your children. How can you model these for your children?

The faith of Timothy's grandmother and mother was so obvious that it was passed from one generation to the next, much like a physical characteristic. Recall times when your faith has been obvious to your children. How real is your faith? (Remember: Real faith doesn't shy away from embracing the realities of life—failures and successes, mistakes and mishaps, doubt and certainty.)

Consider these words from Luke 11:34–36: "If you live wide-eyed in wonder and belief, your body fills up with light. If you live squinty-eyed in greed and distrust, your body is a dank cellar. Keep your eyes open, your lamp burning, so you don't get musty and murky. Keep your life as well-lighted as your best-lighted room" (THE MESSAGE). What does this passage say to you about your faith? Is guilt keeping you from living in "wide-eyed wonder and belief"? Be specific as to how it may be doing this. What can you do with the guilt you're experiencing? What would the mentor you introduced at the beginning of this study say to you about your guilt?

Spend some time talking to God about the guilty feelings you still have, asking him to reveal what is false and should be put away and what is real and should be dealt with.

For You and Your Kids

Preschool–Elementary

Set aside a place in your home for "heroes." Fill a wall or bookshelf with snapshots of those who have influenced you or modeled virtue to you. Include your children's heroes. Talk together about the stories of your heroes. "Try on" their stories and encourage your children to do the same. Tell your children that they are your heroes (perhaps one is especially creative or brave or cheerful), then be sure to include pictures of you and your children in your hero display.

Middle–High School

Before the end of this week, bring your children to visit someone who is in need. Plan together how you will minister to this person's needs. After the visit, talk about the privilege and joy of ministering to others—that it is an outward evidence of inward faith. Identify your child's unique contribution to this experience of service.

All Ages

The most powerful influence you can offer others is a real experience of faith in a real world. You can all exhibit a sincere faith, regardless of economic status, academic degrees, or professional accomplishments. Mothering provides an infinite number of opportunities to *experience* God. The amazing circle of real faith in real life is this: The needs of your children drive them to you; your need to give your children good things drives you to God; God's need to love and care for you provides you with spiritual experiences that you can share with your children; and as you care for your children they receive a taste of God, which makes them hungrier for him.

> *For the first time in months I felt a sense of balance*
> *return. The weight of my deadlines, my illusionary race*
> *with time, my tired and burdened reality.... I didn't need*
> *to reduce the tasks at hand. I didn't need to pour more*
> *sand into the hourglass. All I needed was to remember*
> *what mattered most. Love was the purpose behind*
> *everything. Love for my [children], my family. Love for*

humanity.
Love for God. This was the golden thread of my passion,
the source of my peace and strength—the very conviction
of my soul. This is what made the impossible possible.

FLAVIA AND LISA WEEDN, *ACROSS THE PORCH FROM GOD*

leader's notes

The following notations refer to the questions in the "For You and Others" in each Bible study session. The information included here is intended to give guidance to small group leaders.

session 1:
when guilt is good

During your discussion of the deepest need of the human heart, you can lay the groundwork for a time together that is both vulnerable and supportive. Consider what you could share from your own mothering experience that will encourage others to be vulnerable about their own lives. Transparency is life-giving and confirms that you are related to each other through need and through sweat and tears, that you can be connected with others in order to support some of this world's most important work—mothering!

Question 1.

Mark 2:5, 9—I need to be forgiven.

Luke 7:47-48—I need to be forgiven.

Colossians 2:13—I need to be forgiven!

Question 4. God knows when I sit or stand (verse 2), when I come and go (verse 3), when I speak (verse 4), where I am (verses 8-9), when I try to hide (verse 11), the form of my body (verses 15-16), and what's in my heart (verse 23).

Question 8.

Psalm 13:5 — God's unfailing love

Psalm 18:19 — God's willingness to rescue me and delight in me

Psalm 26:3 — the truth of God's love for me

Psalm 27:13 — God's goodness

Psalm 52:8-9 — God's unfailing love and willingness to make me flourish

Psalm 56:3-4 — God is one who can be trusted and who will protect me

session 2:
if i'm forgiven, why do i feel so bad?

Question 1. Have fun together as you begin this discussion. Share a story from your own mothering when you used a "motherism" or a "martyr motherism." This is a foundational time to talk about how mothers foster false guilt and alienation from one another by not being real.

Perhaps the discussion will flow in the direction of looking at what happens when we make our children our report card instead of enjoying them for who they are. Tape some sounds of children to play for the moms in your group. Talk about the simple joys moms miss when they are consumed with guilt.

Ideas for taping include the following:

- *slurping milk or other mealtime sounds*
- *children calling, "Mommy. Mommy's home!"*
- *children singing*
- *silence (children sleeping)*
- *"I love you, Mom."*

Question 2. God made his love visible when he sent his Son, Jesus.

Question 3. Our love for God is made visible when we love others.

Question 4. God's love for me.

Question 5. Disappointment is something everyone struggles with at some point in life. God is the God of love for the disappointed. He is the only one who will never disappoint.

Question 6. The human tendency is to trust in things we can see and touch and feel. But all of these things will fail us. Only God can be fully trusted to never disappoint.

Question 7. Jesus the Son and God the Father.

Question 8. God, through Jesus, was willing to humble himself all the way to the cross out of love for me.

Question 9. He freely forgives and justifies me through faith in Jesus.

Question 11. God promises to "blot out" — to forget completely the sins I confess to him. I don't have the divine capacity to completely forget. But God does. Whenever I struggle with guilt over past (and forgiven!) sins, the best thing I can do is remember that God forgets!

session 3:
jochebed—let go

Question 1. Role-playing during this discussion could be fun. Imagine yourselves as Israelite women during the time of Jochebed's pregnancy. You could begin the discussion by introducing yourself as Jochebed. Talk about your emotions when you found that you were pregnant during this dangerous time, as well as about your fears for the future.

Question 2. The Israelites remembered where they had come from (Canaan to Egypt), the number of their people when they came (seventy), and the fact that God blessed them by making them grow into a huge nation of Israelites within Egypt.

Question 5. This new king came many years after Joseph had saved the region from famine. The king only knew that the huge number of Israelites—foreigners within his land—posed a security risk for him and the Egyptians. So they made slaves of the Israelites, even going so far as to order that all male babies be killed at birth. When that didn't work, the king ordered that all male babies were to be thrown into the Nile as soon as they were discovered.

Question 6. Bring a stack of current-events magazines to facilitate this discussion. Borrow from neighbors or friends or check them out of a library if you have none of your own.

Question 7. Jochebed could see that her son was special, a "fine child" who had a future other than death in the Nile River. She went to dangerous and extensive lengths to save him from death.

Question 9. She possessed great faith and courage in the face of the king's edict.

Question 10. Consider inviting a mother whose children are grown to share her testimony during this discussion. Interview her during your time together, asking about her experiences of letting go and about her perspective now that her children are grown.

session 4:
deborah—take heart

Question 1. The Israelites did evil in the eyes of the Lord (4:1). The Canaanites came and "cruelly oppressed" them (4:3). In their misery, the Israelites called on God for help (4:3).

Question 3. Deborah was a prophetess, a judge, and a military leader. The only other Bible characters to share these three roles were Moses and Samuel.

Question 4. A "mother in Israel." Deborah had a heart of love and compassion for her people when she saw how much they suffered. But she didn't stop there. She did something about it, following God's leading to go into battle with the Canaanites.

This is a good time to remind your group members that mothering without guilt is not about doing it all perfectly but about living fully as the unique person God created them to be for their children. Share with the group, if appropriate, your own feelings of inadequacy in mothering and how these feelings have been diminished by your partnership with God in parenting.

Question 5. She gave evidence of being wise, since the people trusted in her judgment.

Question 7. She was an influential leader. When Deborah called for Barak to come, he came. When she told him to go, he went.

Question 9. Deborah's deeds are recalled, along with those of other great men and women of faith, thousands of years after they happened.

Question 10. Bring pictures or mementos that represent the influences on your children's lives. Be sure to bring something that symbolizes your own personal influence on your children's lives. As you share sincerely and humbly, you will encourage others that they, too, can be extraordinary influencers in their children's ordinary lives.

Question 11. Nine hundred chariots, cruel, twenty

Question 12. My enemy is the devil. Peter describes him as a roaring lion!

Question 13. She has courage in the face of danger.

Question 15. Deborah had faith that God was with them.

Question 18. Deborah's source of faith and strength was the Lord.

Question 21. Deborah listed all the events of the battle and how God delivered the Israelites. Remembering how God had saved them made the Israelites grateful to God and willing to follow and obey him.

Question 23. By emphasizing the opposite—forgetting God—this verse teaches the importance of remembering God and following him faithfully.

This week, listen closely to your group members, making mental notes of their unique gifts and strengths in mothering. Take the time to send a card or make a telephone call this week to affirm each woman in your group.

session 5:
mary—have faith

Before the group studies this session, go through the entire study, doing all the exercises yourself. Drawing the road map will seem like a daunting task to many, but it is an important component of this study. Draw your own road map. Share with the group your own reluctance in doing this exercise, as well as the benefits you received from it.

Since this session is about Mary and the events of the Christmas season, you may want to set a Christmas atmosphere for your group time. Perhaps you can set up a small Christmas tree, play Christmas music, serve Christmas cookies, and so forth.

Question 1. An angel appeared to Mary (1:26). A child was to be born of a virgin (1:34). Elizabeth was to have a child in her old age (1:36). The baby in Elizabeth's womb recognized Mary (1:41). Mary and Joseph had no place to stay, even though God's Son was about to be born (2:6–7). Angels appeared to a group of shepherds (2:9). Two people in the temple recognized eight-day-old Jesus as the Messiah (2:25, 36). Simeon prophesied that a sword would pierce Mary's soul, and she must have wondered what he meant (2:35).

Question 2. Mary was very young, just engaged, probably around thirteen, fourteen, or fifteen years old. Elizabeth was considerably older, past the years of having children, perhaps in her 50s.

Question 5. Everything that happened had to have confused and scared, and at times delighted, Mary. She was given much to think about.

Question 6.

Luke 1:29—troubled

Luke 1:30—fearful

Luke 1:34—questioning

Luke 1:38—accepting

Luke 2:6—God's Son is born

Luke 2:19—thoughtful, treasuring, and pondering

Luke 2:33—amazed

Luke 2:35—fearful at this prophecy?

Luke 2:48—surprised

Luke 2:50—unclear about what was happening

Luke 2:51—thoughtful

session 6:
lois and eunice—be an example

As you go through this study, decide if it would be beneficial to introduce—in person—your mother mentor to your small group. The introduction can be brief, but it could encourage the women in your group to be thinking about the person who has been influential in their lives.

Question 1. Timothy's mother was a Jew and a believer, while Timothy's father was a Greek and probably not involved in his religious upbringing.

Question 2. His father. Many people come from homes where one parent is uninvolved in their religious upbringing. This reality doesn't preclude a deep religious experience, nor is it an excuse for turning away from God.

Question 3. A sincere faith was handed down from Timothy's grandmother to his mother, then to Timothy himself.

Question 4. God gives useful spiritual gifts to his followers (1:5). A sincere faith is powerful, loving, self-disciplined (1:7). It is never ashamed of the truth and not afraid of suffering for it (1:8). A sincere faith is exhibited in a holy lifestyle (1:9) and made possible by God's grace (1:9). God guards those who have a sincere faith (1:12). The Holy Spirit lives in them (1:14).

Question 5. The Bible doesn't say exactly what these prophecies declared about Timothy, but we can assume they had something to do with his gifts and his call into ministry.

Question 6. A capacity for devoted love and a persistent spirit.

Question 7. Many seemed to think he was very young for such a strong faith and for such significant gifts. Obviously, God thought he was just the right age!

Question 8. An example to others.

Question 9.

1 Timothy 4:13—he should publicly read and teach the Scriptures

1 Timothy 4:14 — he shouldn't neglect his spiritual gifts

1 Timothy 4:15 — he should give himself wholeheartedly to others

1 Timothy 4:16 — he should live carefully and pay close attention to his doctrine

1 Timothy 6:20 — he should watch his speech and guard against false teaching

2 Timothy 2:22 — he should run away from the evil desires of youth and run instead toward righteousness

2 Timothy 2:23 — he shouldn't get involved in foolish arguments

2 Timothy 2:24 — he shouldn't be quarrelsome

2 Timothy 2:25 — he should gently teach those who oppose him

Question 10. The Bible.

CPSIA information can be obtained at www.ICGtesting.com
Printed in the USA
LVOW121914240812

295718LV00001B/2/P